SUCCEEDING
IN YOUR SANDBOX

SUCCEEDING IN YOUR SANDBOX

A STRAIGHTFORWARD GUIDE
TO BEING A GREAT "BOSS"

Communicating • Interacting • Hiring • Onboarding

Setting Goals • Leading/Managing • Delegating

Providing Feedback • Coaching • Consequencing

Developing A Group • Building A Team • Presenting

Handling Conflict • Facilitating Change • Producing Fulfillment

Promoting, Transferring, Terminating

MICHAEL CRYSTAL

ISBN 978-0-557-34109-2

Those who know <u>do</u>.

Those who know more <u>do better</u>.

Those who can best apply what they know <u>excel</u>.

FOREWORD: A TRUE ENCOUNTER

"Michael, it's great to see you again."

"You too, Heather. How are things in the sandbox?"

"Rough as usual what with the volatility, the constant changes and the questions that everyone's been asking regarding the future. We need to find a means to get people really engaged, inspired and committed, regardless of the ups and downs."

"Perhaps it's time to get back to basics."

"Basics?"

"Yes, basics. Making certain that you're really communicating with everyone. Making certain that you're carefully assessing talent. Making certain that people are onboarded properly. Making certain they're really clear regarding their goals and the organization's expectations. Making certain that you and your colleagues are being empathetic, providing lots of coaching, and appropriately using consequences to reinforce the desired behaviors and eradicate the undesired ones. Making certain that you're providing people with meaningful feedback and appraisals of their performance. And all the while focusing on enhancing fulfillment so as to drive and sustain performance."

"Back to basics! Makes a hell of a lot of sense. Thanks! By the way, I don't suppose you have a book that we could use to ensure that we cover them all?"

TABLE OF CONTENTS

INTRODUCTION

According to Sol Price, a legend in the retail world, "Business breaks down into three categories – people, product and facilities – and the same six rules apply to them all: You've got to have the right kind, in the right place, at the right time, in the right quantity, in the right condition, at the right price."

This book is not going to provide you with anything of value regarding product and facilities; however, it will provide you with everything you need to be your best regarding supervising people in your sandbox.

It is a compilation of everything I have learned, taught, observed, applauded and rejected while working with thousands of people, in hundreds of sandboxes, during the last thirty-plus years.

It cuts through the theories and presents what you should do to be the most efficient and effective "boss" you can be, no matter the size or type of your sandbox.

It accounts for everything that will be expected of you by those who you will supervise, direct or otherwise influence.

If you're an experienced "boss," it may reaffirm/enhance what you are already doing, or inspire you to get back to doing what you should be doing.

If you are not yet "in charge" it will provide you with the proper foundation to ensure you will do the right things right.

Think of this book as though it were the content of a training program or a coaching regimen – modules to be learned, applied and woven into the fabric of how you produce sustainable results.

To get the most out of the book, keep in mind:

- Education provides you with knowledge.

- The application of that knowledge develops skill.

- The continuous application of the right knowledge (what Geoff Colvin calls "deliberate practice" in <u>Talent Is Overrated</u>) produces conscious competency, and ultimately subconscious competency: the ability and willingness to consistently do the right things right.

As you conclude each chapter, literally take a few moments to ask and answer the following questions:

1)   "What should I start doing, stop doing or do differently?"

2)   "What effect(s) do I expect from these actions?"

3)   "How will I know if the desired effect(s) are being realized?"

While the world of work is forever changing, there are, and will always be, certain fundamental skills that every "boss" should employ… "Succeeding in Your Sandbox" is your guide to ensuring you'll be able to do those things, and do them right!

ESTABLISHING GREAT RELATIONSHIPS

Did you ever stop and think about why it is that you seemingly get along better with some people than you do with others?

Simply stated, it's all about COMFORT, TRUST and RESPECT.

COMFORT is the myriad feelings you experience when you meet and engage with others.

When you attend an event, and you meet someone for the first time, your "comfort meter" is immediately engaged: You could be totally comfortable with this person, totally uncomfortable, neutral, or anywhere in-between.

Comfort is sort of like "like" (more on this in a moment). It's simply your first (and perhaps lasting) impression, often based on what you can see, hear, feel, think and perceive.

If you're more comfortable than uncomfortable, and decide you may want to interact further, you'll begin to assess the degree or level of TRUST and RESPECT you have for him/her.

TRUST is all about **intent**.

If you see this person to be operating with positive intent – behaving in a fashion that is consistent with your values, beliefs, norms, experiences and perceptions – then you're more inclined to trust him/her.

Trust is often not easily earned, yet all too often can be easily lost.

If you're seen as someone who:

- follows through on commitments
- maintains confidences
- directly addresses individuals with whom there is conflict
- listens respectfully
- accepts others without judgment or question
- seeks and considers opposing viewpoints
- behaves consistently and predictably over time
- acts in a way that matches others' expressed values
- willingly shares information
- shows respect for others' views during disagreements
- demonstrates sensitivity and tact
- involves others in problem-solving and decision-making
- communicates clearly to minimize misunderstanding
- works to solve problems rather than to assign blame
- gives credit to others when warranted
- encourages open discussion of differences of opinion
- values input from others regardless of position
- is open to influence
- admits mistakes and lack of knowledge
- approaches conflict collaboratively
- remains non-defensive when met with disagreement
- requests help when it is needed

then you are quite likely to be perceived to be trustworthy, which leads people to trust you.

RESPECT is all about **value**.

If you see that this person can provide you with something – an idea, a product or service, a sense of well being, a direction worth following – then you're inclined to respect him/her.

Value, like trust, is measured by perception, and perception is reality in the eyes of the perceiver.

If you provide feedback to someone in your sandbox, which is perceived to be critical and overly judgmental rather than developmental and helpful, the value of the feedback, regardless of your intent, is likely to be negative.

If you want to be invited to play in the sandbox, even if it's only for the short-term, then create comfort amongst others by behaving in a fashion that is consistent with the rules of the sandbox.

If you want to successfully lead/manage the sandbox, then allow the people there to share the rules already in place, and work in concert to bring about change only if you believe it is absolutely necessary.

Once comfort has been established, then behave in a fashion – CONSISTENTLY – that clearly exhibits your ability and willingness to always operate with positive intent, and deliver what value you can, on time, in a fashion that maximizes the benefits for others.

So often in the course of my work I've been asked, "To be a successful 'boss,' do people have to like me, and/or, do I have to like them?"

"Like" is an interesting term in the context of a sandbox relationship. In a literal sense, when one "likes" another it is indicative of being fond of that person, enjoying his/her company, and being partial to him/her.

Although desirable, success in the sandbox does not require this sort of palpable connection (in fact, I have known some noteworthy sandboxers who consciously avoided "like" because of possible complications).

Fact is, for the vast majority of you, it's not about being liked.

It's really about people being comfortable with you, and you with them, trusting and respecting each other.

It's all about developing a sustainable relationship that allows you to perform to the best of your ability, and realize the fulfillment that comes from your individual and collective success.

Without comfort, trust and respect, your ability to communicate, influence, lead, manage and successfully engage in all the other necessary activities that "bosses" engage in will be difficult at best.

In my experience I have met and worked with a great number of technically competent individuals whose roles and careers were stymied by their inability (or in some cases unwillingness) to attend to what were once described as the "soft skills."

Yet, as more recent exploration and research has evidenced, it is these "soft skills" that have clearly led to greater individual and collective success.

As you proceed to learn/enhance the "basics" that are illuminated in the chapters that follow, never lose sight of one fundamental truth: without a solid foundation, built of mutual comfort, trust and respect you have for others, and they have for you, your ability to reap the benefits of the skills, tools and methods contained herein will be compromised.

☑ **Behave appropriately to develop comfort**

☑ **Exhibit positive intent to build trust**

☑ **Add value to engender respect**

Those who know do.

Those who know more do better.

Those who can best apply what they know excel.

What should I start doing, stop doing, do differently?

What effect(s) do I expect from these actions?

How will I know if the expected effect(s) occur?

COMMUNICATING REALLY WELL

B eing a great communicator is all about being a great conveyor as well as a great listener.

Being a great communicator requires you to truly understand yourself and others.

Understanding people, others as well as ourselves, begins with comprehending how your own internal communication process works.

First, there's your attitude – how you think and feel about others, which stems from your:

- past experiences *("I enjoy conversing with younger people")*
- beliefs *("People who are well-educated are definitely smarter")*
- values *("Listening is the most important skill in communicating")*
- norms *("I never finish another person's sentence")*
- perceptions *("I enjoy people who dress in classy, stylish attire").*

Next your attitude is transformed into behavior (how you act or react to things) with the help of your "self-talk."

ATTITUDE >>>> *SELF-TALK* >>>> **BEHAVIOR**

How you think and feel	Reinforce?	How you exhibit your
	Change?	thoughts and feelings

Self-talk is that omnipresent, all too often unconscious conversation that goes on inside your head, the one that translates your attitude (how you think and feel about things) into your behavior (how you act and react).

It's that sotto voce that speaks to you, sometimes more frequently than you may realize, not telling you "Breathe, breath, breathe," but telling you "I like, dislike or am neutral about the person with whom I'm communicating."

Once your attitude, being guided by your self-talk, translates itself into behavior, you quite naturally then find yourself communicating effectively and efficiently, or ineffectively and inefficiently.

In my experience with great communicators, there is clearly a difference; when I've queried them as to what makes them consistently more efficient and effective they seem to have more ability and willingness to accommodate the similarities and differences that they may have with whom they communicate.

Upon further observation I discovered that accommodation is not only behavioral, it's definable: the ability and willingness to…

- go into situations without preconceived notions: being **flexible**

- listen and respond without prejudice: being **open-minded**

- attempt and do many things: being **versatile**

- shift direction as may be necessary: being **adaptable**

- get outside your own paradigm: being **changeable**

- incorporate others' points of view: being **negotiable**

- deal with adversity and challenge: being **tolerant**

- be empathetic or sympathetic: being **outwardly focused**.

These are all learned behaviors, things that you can train yourself to do in every situation to make you a better communicator.

Furthermore, to the extent you're seen as being able and willing to exhibit these behaviors more frequently and consistently than not, those with whom you communicate have a greater tendency to reciprocate.

Accommodation suggests that you behave like a thermostat instead of a thermometer when communicating with others – rather than simply taking a measure of the temperature, adjust the temperature so that you and others are the most comfortable you can be.

Being accommodating to others helps you to ultimately achieve your own objectives.

If you help those with whom you communicate be more comfortable, they're more likely to "buy" from you (since 90% of all buying decisions are emotionally-driven).

It's quite natural that most people set their "interpersonal thermostats" at a level that allows them to be comfortable.

Yet if you intend to interact in a way that will facilitate the interaction, then you must choose to adjust your thermostat accordingly.

Of course, each of you will adjust your setting depending on a variety of factors and variables, some of which are in your control and some of which are imposed by others.

Allowing for these vast differences, and recognizing that no one approach is going to be successful with everyone, your success in any interaction will be the direct result of your willingness and ability to consistently make others feel more comfortable with you.

As I stated earlier, being a great communicator requires you to be as great a listener as you may be a conveyor.

Marshall Goldsmith, in an article published in *Fast Company* magazine in July, 2005 describes an encounter in Sparks Steakhouse between a young lawyer and David Boies, one of the country's most renowned lawyers:

"...I wasn't bowled over by his intelligence, or his piercing questions, or his anecdotes. What impressed me was that when he asked a question, he waited for the answer. He not only listened, he made me feel like I was the only person in the room."

When was the last time that anyone described your listening skills that way?

Those of you who can readily utilize the physiological ability to hear don't always realize there is a difference between hearing and listening; yet, listening is really a psychological skill.

To truly be a great communicator, you must employ your ability and willingness to first attend to the person with whom you're communicating.

Next, you need to process and understand the messages he/she is conveying.

Then, most importantly, you must respond in a way that clearly indicates you've really listened.

Attending is all about being there for that other person – not just hearing him/her while you're otherwise looking out the window, or grabbing that ringing phone, or the worst, playing with your PDA.

Next, processing and understanding comes from the ability to absorb not only what is being said, but how it's being said – the tone of voice and the nonverbal body language providing much more of the message.

According to Professor Albert Mehrabian at UCLA, 7% of meaning is in the words that are spoken, 38% of meaning is paralinguistic (the way that the words are said) and 55% of meaning is in facial expression.

You process to understand enthusiasm, urgency, disgust, joy, melancholy, regret, excitement and the myriad other "pieces of music" that accompany the words you're listening to.

Lastly, there's the meaningful response: whatever has been conveyed is acknowledged, regardless of the reaction you may be experiencing or about to convey.

It's not that you are necessarily agreeing or disagreeing, but you have really listened and are now ready to continue to communicate.

ATTENDING • PROCESSING • RESPONDING

To be a truly great listener, you will want to make certain that your self-talk volume is lowered, lest you end up listening more to yourself than the other person; additionally, you will want to:

- tune out any distractions
- avoid interrupting other people
- never change subjects without warning
- evidence a sincere interest in the discussion
- avoid jumping to conclusions
- let people finish their own sentences
- stay focused at all times
- maintain eye contact
- never have someone repeat himself/herself unnecessarily.

In my experience I've all too often heard individuals complain "our basic problem is we're not communicating," and when I've asked, "What exactly does that mean?" the responses I typically received were always the same: "He/she/they aren't clear when they talk to us" and/or "he/she/they don't listen well at all."

Asking, "Why do you think that's occurring?" I often was told, "I/we don't know," which led me to conclude the symptoms were easily recognizable but few could find the underlying cause.

Yet, there's got to be cause!

Great communicators are made, not born (although there's no denying that some people are naturally gifted at conveying, or listening, or both), and your skills are honed through continuous assessment, feedback, modification and more practice.

If there's a lack of clarity in someone's conveyance, take the time to ensure the communication process doesn't end before you receive whatever you need (e.g., more details re: the present, the future, the desired results, the effect on the team) to lift the fog.

If what you've heard is not 100% clear to you, make certain you do a check for understanding before the communication process ends, lest you end up doing the WRONG things.

In summary, there's no good reason for poor communication!

☑ *Learn how to be a thermostat*

☑ *Get in touch with your self-talk*

☑ *It's not what you say, it's what others hear/infer*

Those who know do.

Those who know more do better.

Those who can best apply what they know excel.

What should I start doing, stop doing, do differently?

What effect(s) do I expect from these actions?

How will I know if the expected effect(s) occur?

SELECTING THE BEST TALENT

Every time I've conducted a workshop on interviewing and selection skills, no less than 20% of the audience has come right up to me at the conclusion and said, "Where were you 20 years ago when I really needed you?"

Most people really do believe that interviewing and selecting talent is not a learnable skill set.

Worse still, most people still rely more on how they feel about a candidate than on whether or not the candidate possesses the balance of ability, willingness and fit that will likely make him/her best suited to the job, the sandbox and the environment.

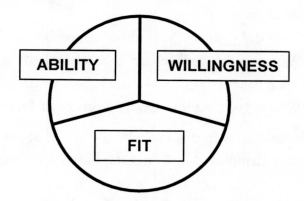

I'm not denying the gut feelings that are inherent in the process (remember, I'm the one who said it's all about "comfort" when it comes to playing nice in the sandbox).

In fact, I've always told people, "As the interview is drawing to a close, ask yourself, if this candidate were to end up at my #1 competitor's company tomorrow morning, how would I feel?" If the answer is anything less than "horrible," ask yourself why?

Regardless of what his/her resume contains, or what the candidate may state, the means by which you can best minimize the risks associated with hiring is to remember that past performance is the best predictor of future performance.

Every question you ask should be couched in a historical perspective. For example, if you ask a candidate, "How would you intend to lead the team that would be yours?" he/she can too easily provide you with a textbook answer.

Therefore you should ask the candidate to:

- "Tell me about a time when you were responsible for other's performance."
- "How did you obtain the role?"
- "What exactly did you do?"
- "What did you (not the team) accomplish?"
- "What was the feedback from those you led?"
- "What benefit did you gain from this experience?"
- "What did you like least (and/or most) about this experience?"

By asking the questions in this manner, you're apt to get a whole lot more factual information and make a better hiring decision.

Frame a relevant experience

Affirm the actions taken

Confirm the outcomes

Talk about the take-aways

By Framing a relevant experience, Affirming the specific actions taken and Confirming the results/outcomes of these actions, the candidate provides evidence of his/her ability. By Talking about the take-aways (his/her feelings), the candidate provides valuable insight into his/her willingness to perform in the future, and the fit with how things are done in your sandbox.

I'm not implying that people don't have the capacity to grow and develop in the job; that they have to possess <u>all</u> of the requisite skills to perform well; that they may not experience increased motivation once their employment commences.

But hiring a less than qualified person – one who doesn't possess the necessary skill (ability), motivation (willingness) and attributes (fit) – poses risks and costs that are simply too great.

When making your selection decision:

- judge both the depth and breadth of each candidate's experience (remember, there's a big difference between *20 years of experience* and *1 year of experience 20 times over*)

- make certain there's clear evidence that he/she is motivated to do what's required by the job and the sandbox's culture

- be sure he/she has the ability and willingness to create and sustain comfort, trust and respect with the sandbox's existing population.

If I had to choose what's most important – ability, willingness or fit – I'd have to say fit since you can more readily increase and improve the first two, whereas a lack of fit is more difficult to correct.

If the new hire has never experienced a fast-paced, bare knuckles environment like the one in your sandbox, or is coming from an environment where individual contributors thrived, and your sandbox is all about teamwork, he/she is likely to experience rapidly diminishing fulfillment, and even a quick departure, when he/she or you all too quickly realizes there's no fit.

In summary, the selection of talent is never to be taken lightly. Given the extraordinary cost of "bad hires" (estimated by some at more than $100,000 on average), in addition to the aggravation that everyone experiences, selecting the best talent for every position is critical for success.

☑ **Only hire those who are able, willing and will fit**

☑ **Past experience is better than potential**

☑ **Proven results are more valuable than activities**

Those who know do.

Those who know more do better.

Those who can best apply what they know excel.

What should I start doing, stop doing, do differently?

What effect(s) do I expect from these actions?

How will I know if the expected effect(s) occur?

ONBOARDING: A MUST FOR ALL NEWCOMERS

One of the great mistakes made in so many sandboxes is the failure to properly on-board new members.

To have spent the extraordinary time, effort, energy and money to hire the best and the brightest, only to then afford them a hasty introduction into the sandbox, so often sets the wrong tone and gets people off on the wrong foot.

In the worst case I've heard, a very talented, highly experienced new hire was welcomed by his two new colleagues with <u>210</u> "To Dos" e-mailed over to his mailbox. When their "boss," who was cc'd, asked, "Why?" she was told "Well, he's here now, he's got lots of experience and we thought he'd like to jump right in and get started." Needless to say, this welcome to the sandbox almost resulted in a rather quick departure.

More than the perfunctory welcome that's most often provided by someone from the HR Department, I'm referring here to the kind of welcome that exhibits respect and immediately gives the person the feeling that his/her arrival has been eagerly anticipated, and those already in the sandbox are really happy that he/she is finally onboard.

To best ensure they're properly assimilated, be prepared to provide the new hire with answers to the following regarding the team/function/department:

- where do we come from?   our history

- what are we good at?   our strengths

- how are we different?   our uniqueness

- whom do we serve?   our customers

- how do we act?   our behaviors

- what do we believe in?   our values

- why do we do what we do?   our purpose

Additionally, "bosses" should provide every new arrival with a clear understanding of how things work regarding taking risks, empowerment, creativity, dealing with success/failure, pursuing opportunities and solving problems, and should outline every expectation against which the new hire will likely be measured.

Bottom-line, the more the new hire is made aware of upon arrival into the sandbox, the less likely it is that he/she will fail to meet the needs, wants and expectations of those already in residence.

☑ **Get people assimilated quickly**

☑ **Make certain they know all the rules**

☑ **Forge a community**

Those who know do.

Those who know more do better.

Those who can best apply what they know excel.

What should I start doing, stop doing, do differently?

What effect(s) do I expect from these actions?

How will I know if the expected effect(s) occur?

SETTING GOALS AND EXPECTATIONS

Simply stated, goals are the metrics describing what's to be done.

In my experience virtually everyone has been exposed to the SMART model for setting [S]pecific, [M]easurable, [A]ctionable, [R]ealistic, [T]ime-bound goals. Yet, like any time-honored model, enhancements often make it more valuable:

- Succinct
- Motivational
- Aligned
- Relevant
- Trackable

Goals need to be short, sweet and crisp. They need to inspire the person who's attempting to achieve them. They need to be in sync with all other individual and collective goals. They need to be germane to the mission and purpose of the whole of the sandbox, and their progress needs to be easily assessed as the path to success is traveled.

Over the years I've often noted the contradiction that existed in most of the sandboxes to which I was invited: everyone seemed willing to acknowledge that when people were allowed to participate in the creation of their own goals, they'd be more likely to pursue their achievement with energy and vigor.

Yet most "bosses" prescribed goals in a fashion that led people to compliance, putting in only the time necessary to achieve the minimum desirable outcome.

Why???

In my view, laziness. It's easier to simply tell someone what to do than it is to engage in a dialogue that will undoubtedly take more time and may instill the notion that the person on the receiving end may actually have a stake in what's being planned.

If goals are to be SMART, then be smart in how you produce them!

Goals generally tell you what you need to do, yet when they're written properly they should also tell you how they should be achieved – that is, the goal should describe any particular behavior(s) that will enhance the chances for success.

The failure to describe the need to "engage the entire team" while attempting to "achieve your goal" could result in success for the individual while creating all sorts of sandbox relations problems.

One of the most common problems that poor goal/expectation-setting produces is the argument that occurs when the rating of one's performance versus the goal is seen differently by the rater and the doer.

Yet if the measures of "meets expectations" and "exceeds expectations" are clearly defined at the time the goal was set, the need for debate all but disappears.

Another problem stems from the inability to develop a clear "line of sight" between goals, whether viewed vertically or horizontally.

I recall conducting a "how to set goals" workshop and having the company's receptionist state, "I just don't see how my achieving my goals will affect the company's achieving a goal of increasing sales by 30%."

Before I could even acknowledge her concern, three participants gave her vivid examples of how her not meeting her goals for handling calls and visitors could readily affect the company's meeting or not meeting its revenue goal.

Yet another problem that I see frequently is a goal/expectation that requires someone else achieving his or her goal first.

Again, with the intent of avoiding unnecessary consternation at the time performance is reviewed, allowing for the contingency in the initial setting of the goal/expectation should all but eliminate unnecessary excuses if the doer fails to meet the objective.

It's critical for success that all parties clearly understand not only what needs to be achieved, but also how it needs to be achieved, if optimal success is to be realized.

So often in my experience, post-mortems done on missed goals have provided clear evidence that the absence of truly understanding (1) what was supposed to get done, and (2) the ways it was supposed to be done, have been the greatest causes of failure.

So whether you ask someone to play back to you his/her understanding, or have them recap what their plan of action might be, or have them send you an e-mail recapping the discussion, or the receiving party simply provides it voluntarily, make certain a clear understanding exists!

> ☑ *Make sure everyone knows where you're going*
>
> ☑ *Make certain the "line of sight" is clear*
>
> ☑ *Know the measures of "met" before you start*

Those who know do.

Those who know more do better.

Those who can best apply what they know excel.

What should I start doing, stop doing, do differently?

```

```

What effect(s) do I expect from these actions?

```

```

How will I know if the expected effect(s) occur?

```

```

LEADING AND MANAGING

L et me begin with a blanket statement (it's my book, so I get to do that): Too much has been made over the years about what management is, what leadership is, and when do you engage in one or the other.

If you want to be successful in every type of sandbox, you have to be good at both!

In Leaders *(Harper and Row, 1985),* the authors Warren Bennis and Burt Nanus tell us "Managers are people who do things right, and leaders are people who do the right things."

Why would I want to be in a sandbox with someone whose doing one or the other yet not both?!

Leadership	**Management**
Vision	Mission
Strategies	Tactics
Recognition	Rewards
Fulfillment	Performance
Transformations	Transactions
Future	Present
People	Process

Do them all, do them right, and everyone in the sandbox wins.

"But more specifically, how can I be the best '"boss"'?" you ask.

"By leading/managing in ways people want to be led/managed."

Rather than struggling with all the models and tactics, trying to figure out which one is best, and which one to use, simply ask everyone, "How would you like me to lead/manage you?" and then agree to do it just that way, <u>AS LONG AS HE/SHE MEETS OR EXCEEDS GOALS AND EXPECTATIONS</u>.

If by chance, he/she doesn't, then be prepared to lead/manage him/her in the way you otherwise think is best, with the incentive of going back to the more desirable way once performance has improved.

Leading/managing is all about getting the right things done, correctly and on time.

It's in great measure all about engaging "followers" through influence (the use of your personal power) rather than your positional authority.

If you want people to cooperate with you in your endeavors, help them to commit their time and energy, rather than forcing them to comply with your dictates.

Give them every opportunity to do it their way, as long as you're making certain that goals are being achieved, deadlines are being met and quality remains high.

Compliance gets you 75-90% performers; commitment gets you 95-120% performers. Get what you need from people by allowing them to get what they want from you, and keep it simple:

- Empower people who are capable and committed
- Teach people who are committed but not yet capable
- Motivate people who are capable yet not committed
- Micro-manage people who are incapable and uncommitted

CAPABLE

MOTIVATE	**EMPOWER**
UNCOMMITTED	*COMMITTED*
MICRO-MANAGE	**TEACH**

INCAPABLE

Capability and commitment know no bounds regarding age and style, yet adjusting your approach to leading/managing people based on their age and style is critical to your success.

LEADING/MANAGING DIFFERENT GENERATIONS

Let's begin with people's ages, or as it is often referred to, their "generations."

Traditionalists, born between 1925-1942, are generally described as stable, detail-oriented, thorough, loyal, hard working and live by the rules types.

To best lead/manage them, show respect for their experience and loyalty, and allow them to build a legacy as they move to the natural end of their careers.

Next there are the Boomers, born between 1943-1960, generally described as service oriented, driven, willing to go the extra mile, good at relationships and liking to work on teams.

To best lead/manage them, provide them with opportunities to develop challenging career paths, affording them more visibility and the chance to excel.

Next there are the GenXers, born between 1961-1981, generally described as adaptable, techno-literate, independent, results-oriented (in a recent survey of workers in this generation, 45% of those asked thought it "a good idea to fire the bottom tenth of performers each year"), unintimidated by authority and seeking to exhibit creativity.

To best lead/manage them, allow them to feel as though their careers are moving forward at all times (figuratively, not literally), with new paths of growth and development (even though they're in the same role/position) being provided regularly.

Lastly (at least for the moment), there are the Millenials, also known as GenYers, born between 1981-1989, generally described as optimistic, multi-taskers, technologically savvy and spirited.

To best lead/manage them, provide them with lots of coaching (that's what they've been used to growing up), and opportunities to engage in as many activities and tasks as can be reasonably handled so they're always building multi-faceted parallel careers.

Like any characterization or classification, don't view people's ages as being an absolute indicator of their generations. Listen for the words and the tone, and observe the behavior, before assigning a label to anyone. Even then, be attentive to the results of your efforts, and be prepared to adjust your application of the suggested approaches, regardless of a person's chronological age.

LEADING/MANAGING DIFFERENT STYLES

Regarding any individual's working style (defined as his/her behavior), the most commonly used descriptors of the four major characterizations are: Amiable, Analytical, Driver, Expressive.

These styles do not reflect an individual's 'personality' (e.g., introversion or extraversion), but rather the ways in which they go about doing their job (or living their lives), with no natural connection to one's age.

Amiables are generally seen as being passive and warm, loyal, patient and caring (think of Nelson Mandela, JK Rowling, Jennifer Aniston), and are best led/managed in a compromising fashion, where the emphasis is on teamwork and collaboration.

Analyticals are generally seen as being passive and cool, studious and attentive to details (think of Bill Gates, Jodie Foster, Albert Einstein), and are best led/managed in a way that allows them to take the time to ensure accuracy and quality (yet not miss the required deadline).

Drivers are generally seen as being assertive and cool, results-driven and fast-paced (think of Jack Welch, Martha Stewart, Tom Hanks), and are best led/managed by being allowed to work autonomously (assuming they possess the required skill), while contributing to the solution of a defined problem.

Expressives are generally seen as being assertive and warm, resourceful and determined (think of Ellen Degeneres, Richard Branson, Barack Obama), and are best led/managed by being allowed to be creative and engaged in many projects simultaneously.

Amongst the thousands of individuals who I've observed:

- only 5% I assessed constantly behaved in a way that allows me to characterize them as exhibiting only 1 of the 4 styles
- 70% often exhibited characteristics of 2 of the 4 styles
- 15% exhibited 3 of the 4
- 10% exhibited all 4 of the 4 in relative balance.

Assess what you're seeing and hearing, be prepared for people to shift their style, and be prepared to shift with them.

In my experience – and I've had the good fortune to be in the presence of, and worked with a number of very well-known and highly successful leader/managers – they rarely, if ever, exhibited an imbalance between leading and managing.

In fact, more often than not, the two were seamlessly transparent, being utilized in interdependent ways, producing far more willingness to really pitch in amongst those whose engagement was critical to the sandbox's success.

In summary, leading/managing, rather than leading or managing, has you focusing on the entire situation, balanced in your view and your approach (e.g., tactical AND strategic; people AND process; bottom line AND top line), allowing you to ensure higher levels of sustainable success.

> ☑ *Lead AND Manage, not lead OR manage*
>
> ☑ *Rely on influence, not positional authority*
>
> ☑ *Gain commitment, more than just compliance*

Those who know do.

Those who know more do better.

Those who can best apply what they know excel.

What should I start doing, stop doing, do differently?

What effect(s) do I expect from these actions?

How will I know if the expected effect(s) occur?

DELEGATING PRODUCES MORE RESULTS

In the previous chapter I described the "boss's" role as primarily producing results through others, while actually doing the things only he/she should be doing.

To even begin to approach this allocation, you must be both able and willing to delegate.

Delegate in a purposeful, correct way.

Don't drop and run.

Don't abdicate.

Don't forget, you're transferring responsibility, not accountability.

In my experience most "bosses" don't delegate anywhere near as often or as much as they could or should, most often because they don't want to take the time to teach, or they fear that the task will not be done as well or on time.

Yet when asked, they readily acknowledge that they don't want to be doing as much of the work as they're doing, and they do want to provide opportunities for team members to learn, grow and develop.

When done correctly – well-planned, properly executed and consistently reviewed and supported – the vast majority of delegated tasks are completed just as though they were done by the delegator, with the by-product of enabling and empowering others.

First, the plan for delegating a task has to be developed.

It must include a thorough analysis of the *what* (the task) and the *who* (the person/people), but not necessarily the *how*.

The task must be thoroughly defined (outcomes, quality, timeframes), and the person should be vetted as to his/her ability and willingness (<u>both</u> must be rated "high"), and availability.

Next, a meeting with the chosen person/people to initiate the assignment need be scheduled.

It should include a thorough description of the "what," a disclosure as to the rationale for choosing him/her/them, and a very clear description of how much authority they have.

"Do the work and review it with me before sending it along" versus "Do the work, send it along to everyone and let me know what sort of feedback you receive" are quite different.

Without a clear understanding of how much authority you've delegated to the person(s) doing the task, the ultimate effect on you, the delegator, can be vastly different than you expected, and potentially disastrous.

Then lastly, and most often overlooked, is the follow-up that ensures that the delegated task has a higher probability of being properly completed.

Be sure to schedule review meetings coincidental with the work schedule/milestones.

Also be sure to check-in with the person/people, informally, to simply see how they're doing.

When done in this fashion, delegation can readily produce more results for you and others, with the added benefit of helping others increase their fulfillment from work by learning new skills and enhancing their career possibilities.

Additionally, for you, the development of some "bench strength" may prove to be very valuable when you're next being considered for promotion.

In summary, if you're looking for the means to getting more involved in new and perhaps more invigorating opportunities, yet don't want to risk the undesired drop-off in the expected productivity of your sandbox, delegate more!

☑ **If you want it done right then delegate it properly**

☑ **Delegation = Opportunity**

☑ **Plan; Initiate; Follow-up**

Those who know do.

Those who know more do better.

Those who can best apply what they know excel.

What should I start doing, stop doing, do differently?

What effect(s) do I expect from these actions?

How will I know if the expected effect(s) occur?

PROVIDING FEEDBACK IS A "MUST DO"

Shockingly, according to a study produced by Harvard's Business School, 80% of a surveyed population could not accurately describe how well or poorly they were performing on the job based on feedback provided by those responsible for their performance!

People DO want to know how they're doing!

In fact, even those who may be failing miserably want to know, sooner rather than later, in the off chance they might actually be able to correct some of their failings before the dreaded performance appraisal is delivered.

If you don't tell poor performers they're performing poorly, they have every reason to go home at night thinking things are fine, and therefore may keep performing poorly.

If you don't tell good performers they're performing well, they may have every reason to go home at night feeling they're not being recognized for what they're doing well, and their performance may begin to slip over time.

Even in the busiest sandboxes there are likely to be myriad times to informally provide feedback.

When you catch someone doing something correctly, or when you're assisting someone who you notice is struggling, or when you've learned that someone is not performing up to expectations – these are all moments in which the provision of feedback, delivered in a timely, developmental way, can have a significantly positive effect.

In more formal sandboxes, performance appraisals are the customary means for providing feedback, and most appraisers with whom I've come in contact rue their existence.

The forms are too complicated and lengthy.

The language you're required to use is too formulaic.

The forced rankings and distribution of rankings to match up with the salary plan are too encumbering.

The discussions that are supposed to take place are seemingly more about fulfilling the sandbox's policy requirements than they are about really helping people grow and develop.

If you want your performance appraisal preparations to be easier, collect more data more frequently.

If you want your performance appraisal discussions to be easier, provide more feedback on a timely basis.

If you want the effects of a performance appraisal to be more noticeable, offer more suggestions on how to be even better.

If you engage in a fair number of coaching conversations, the formal appraisal will be nothing more than a summary of what's otherwise already been discussed regarding effort and results.

But even if you do all the right things right, you may still run up against a "system" that won't allow people to receive an honest rating for the work they've done.

I could literally cite hundreds of examples of people who were flat out told, "I couldn't give you the *superior* rating you deserved because I can only have one of those in my department and I had already given it to someone else in the sandbox."

So, besides not getting the tangible reward that he/she believes has been earned, he/she isn't getting the intangible, and all too important, recognition that is richly deserved.

In whatever way possible, make certain that you afford the "victim(s)" of the "system" as much reinforcement, opportunity and support as you can, lest the effect of being slighted leads to declining fulfillment and performance.

In summary, continuous feedback, in conjunction with meaningful performance appraisals, provide sandboxers with the means for:

- sustaining their high levels of performance
- enhancing their acceptable levels of performance
- correcting their poor levels of performance.

When provided in a timely manner, and a developmental fashion (please forego the use of the words "constructive criticism" since the vast majority of sandboxers only hear the word "criticism"), you'll likely find that performance, and fulfillment, will be better.

☑ **Be more descriptive, less evaluative**

☑ **Acknowledge what was done well**

☑ **Offer what could have been done differently**

Those who know do.

Those who know more do better.

Those who can best apply what they know excel.

What should I start doing, stop doing, do differently?

What effect(s) do I expect from these actions?

How will I know if the expected effect(s) occur?

COACHING BUILDS COMPETENCY

Being a coach is like being a golf caddy.

Sometimes you're there to <u>provide feedback</u>:
GOLFER: "Do you think my game is improving?"
CADDY: "Yes sir, you miss the ball much closer now."

Sometimes you're there to <u>raise awareness</u>:
GOLFER: "That can't be my ball, it's too old."
CADDY: "It's been a long time since we teed off, sir."

Sometimes you're there to <u>challenge</u>:
GOLFER: "I think I'm going to drown myself in the lake."
CADDY: "Think you can keep your head down that long?"

And sometimes you're simply there to <u>provide encouragement</u>:
GOLFER: "Do you think I can get there with a 5 iron?"
CADDY: "Eventually."

Coaching is, in its simplest form, a process of working in partnership with someone to help improve, extend and/or reinforce performance and fulfillment…to assist, without removing responsibility for action.

Coaching has a very specific business purpose: To improve that which is below standard; enhance that which is at standard; and/or sustain that which is exemplary.

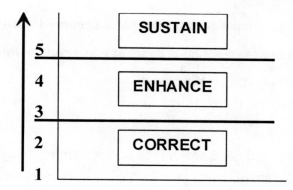

Everyone can benefit from coaching! World-class performers in sports, the arts and the business world all rely on personal coaches to sustain their high level of performance.

Coaching is coaching, and therefore it's not:

- a performance evaluation, since there is no score
- counseling, because it's all about on-the-job performance
- therapy, which is better left to trained professionals
- a monologue, which suggests there's no partnership.

Simply stated, coaching is a process that focuses on people's performance; so…

- If you want to SUSTAIN high performance, use coaching to get people to CONTINUE doing whatever they're doing
- If you want to ENHANCE good performance, use coaching to get people to START doing what they should be doing
- If you want to CORRECT poor performance, use coaching to get people to STOP doing what they're doing (and then start doing what they're supposed to be doing).

In all cases, the content of a coaching conversation should contain:

- an accurate description of **what was expected**

- a detailed description of **what occurred/didn't occur**

- a precise description of **what was produced/not produced.**

The key to good coaching is to always remember the primary objective: helping the recipient to correct, enhance or sustain his/her performance.

The key to being a good coach is to also remember that you don't have to have all the answers, but you do need to have lots of good questions.

In my experience, including lots of time spent with people whose jobs I most certainly could not perform, I found the more questions I posed – questions that were really provocative, penetrating, challenging – the more we achieved in our work together.

Literally forcing the person being coached to deal with the problem, or chase the opportunity, gave cause to better solutions or responses.

Of course, there were times where I might add a suggestion, or even go so far as to propose yet another alternative, but never before the responsible party had a hearty go at it.

Coaching takes time; time is money; yet the measurable increases in performance and fulfillment more than justify the investment.

> ☑ *Partner to help break old (bad) habits*
>
> ☑ *Focus on sustaining, enhancing, correcting*
>
> ☑ *Help people become consciously competent*

Those who know do.

Those who know more do better.

Those who can best apply what they know excel.

What should I start doing, stop doing, do differently?

What effect(s) do I expect from these actions?

How will I know if the expected effect(s) occur?

CONSEQUENCING TO AFFECT BEHAVIOR

Years ago I heard a story attributed to Ferdinand Fournies, an internationally known consultant, author and former teacher at Columbia University's Graduate School of Business.

In a discussion that followed a lecture on how to get people to change their behavior – in essence, how to get them to perform better – a student proffered this problem: the team that he was a member of at the office was the same team that played together in the corporate softball league, and while their individual and collective performance at the office was acceptable, there was little evidence of any desire to materially improve; yet on the field, they seemingly were always looking for ways to do better.

In his one word response, "Consequences," Fournies shed light on one of the most important concepts in leading/managing people's behavior/performance.

People at the office receive meaningful consequences – recognition, rewards, punishment, penalties – that are provided in a somewhat timely fashion perhaps only 2-3 times a year.

On the playing field, every action taken is recognized or rewarded, punished or penalized, instantly, providing immediate gratification (which sustains the performance) or disappointment (which lends itself to correction or enhancement).

Consequences affect behavior!

But they've got to be personal (really felt by those receiving them) and immediate (received as near as possible to whatever called for them).

Promises of a future reward rarely have the same effect as a reward, or even recognition, has when provided on a timely basis.

Threats of punishment or penalty generally produce a state-of-mind that says, "I've got one more chance before anything bad might happen."

Rewards or recognition provided to everyone in the sandbox, yet actually earned by only a few contributors, generally will have a tendency to diminish the commitment level of higher performers.

Punishment or penalties meted out to the entire sandbox not only allows the deserving parties to escape, but certainly casts a negative pale over everyone else.

If you're like most "bosses" you'll be challenged regarding the balancing of rewards and recognition.

Yet balance is just what you're after. In the hundreds of seminars I've conducted where the subject turns to "more money" or "more praise," I found the vast majority of participants want for both in equal doses. In fact, when asked to choose only ten forms of positive reinforcement, out of a list of twenty items (10 + 10), 80% of the group chose 5-5 or 4-6/6-4 for rewards and recognition.

If you're short on ideas for either or both:

- Ask the potential recipients what they'd like (with the understanding that you may not be able to deliver everything).

- Try new and different methods to poll people to get their feedback; then use it to choose what to try next.

- Balance the delivery of the tangible (rewards) with the intangible (recognition) to the greatest extent possible.

If you're uncertain regarding punishments or penalties, consider these real-world examples (all of which should be reviewed to ensure you're not violating any of your sandbox's rules or norms):

- Initiate fact-based conversations, citing specific examples of unacceptable behavior, in which you make the sandboxer aware that, in your view, "he/she is willfully choosing to perform inappropriately."

- Increase the frequency and regularity of formal checks of the sandboxer's work, with immediate feedback and correction if necessary.

- Reset deadlines for work to be done: For example, "this report has to be completed today, and it must be error-free, regardless of the additional time you'll have to spend."

- Assign work you know the sandboxer does not like to do, again with stringent goals (measures of how much, how good and by when).

- Move the sandboxer to a less desirable workspace.

- Deny privileges to attend outside activities that occur during work hours and/or at company expense.

- Demote the sandboxer to a lesser role, and reduce the salary and other forms of compensation commensurately.

- Deny or delay any form of monetary rewards.

- Have the sandboxer work on events that he/she would otherwise attend, yet don't allow them to do so.

- Advise the sandboxer that his/her career path will no longer be included in performance evaluation discussions.

- Have the sandboxer complete a weekly (or even daily) self-assessment of what he/she has done and how well he/she has done it.

- Become a "continuous negative consequence," frequently just showing up in the sandboxer's workspace to check on how things are going.

- As each task/activity that the sandboxer is otherwise desirous of doing is removed, set out clear goals and expectations of what the sandboxer needs to do to get it back.

- If the sandboxer persists in willfully choosing to perform inappropriately have him/her prepare a documented plan for improving the situation.

At all times, remember to mete out negative consequences judiciously, and perhaps only after consulting with your HR professionals to ensure that you're not stepping over the line in a way that will result in a claim of harassment.

Furthermore, remember that the rationale for imposing the consequence is that the individual who is on the receiving end has "earned his or her just desserts."

People who are subjected to negative consequences will often claim that the imposition is unwarranted, and that the imposer is simply being "unfair."

To this you must say, "But if you were receiving a positive consequence you'd undoubtedly believe you earned it, so why can't you accept the fact that you've earned the negative consequence that's being imposed?"

In summary, do your best to always provide as much in the way of positive consequences as possible, continuously recognizing people for their effort and rewarding them for their results.

If and when it may be necessary, utilize negative consequences – punishment or penalty – to ensure that unacceptable, unproductive behavior is eradicated as quickly as possible.

> ☑ *Say "thank you" more often*
>
> ☑ *Continuously recognize effort*
>
> ☑ *Always celebrate and reward results*

Those who know do.

Those who know more do better.

Those who can best apply what they know excel.

What should I start doing, stop doing, do differently?

What effect(s) do I expect from these actions?

How will I know if the expected effect(s) occur?

DEVELOPING A COHESIVE GROUP

Before team building can occur, a foundation must be in place:

Values: what's important around here.

Vision: a collective view of a time somewhere in our future.

Mission: what we need to do to get to our desired future state.

Goals: the measures that tell us how we're doing in our quest.

If people are to work toward achieving what is necessary to sustain the success of the sandbox, then they need to participate in the creation of these four key elements.

Values define the environment in which work gets done.

> "Speed, Simplicity, Self-confidence."
>
> "Profit; Shareholder Value; Growth."
>
> "Personal Health and Well-being."

These are simply examples, and the true values in any collective effort must be articulated and endorsed by the people working in that environment.

Most importantly, they must then be *the walk that everyone walks* and not simply *the talk that everyone talks*.

Vision is powerful.

Peter Drucker, the renowned management consultant, said, "The best way to prepare for the future is to create it."

Vision is about what people want to be, where they want to get to, a desired future state.

In 1961, when John Kennedy spoke of putting a man safely on the moon and returning him to Earth by the end of the decade, he created a powerful vision for the thousands who wanted to participate in such a noteworthy venture.

When Bill Gates said that he sees a world where there'll be a computer on every desk and table, and that his software will be in it, he was articulating a vision that people could (and did) rally around.

Vision gives people hope, inspiration and the motivation to strive for success.

Mission is all about how it is that the values will be upheld and the vision will be realized.

Mission speaks to the overarching way in which people will endeavor to succeed.

"To solve unsolved problems innovatively" *(3M)*

"To give unlimited opportunity to women" *(Mary Kay)*

"To preserve and improve human life" *(Merck)*

"To give ordinary folk the chance to buy
the same thing as rich people" *(Wal-Mart)*

"To make people happy" *(Disney)*

Succinct, clear statements that tell everyone what needs be done, in the broadest sense, to reach that desired future state.

Goals are the metrics and benchmarks that provide the direction for the strategies and tactics that need to be employed if the values, vision and mission are to be realized.

As Andy Grove, Intel's founder said, "If you don't know where you're going, any road will get you there."

Without SMART (Specific and Succinct; Measurable and Motivational; Achievable and Aligned; Realistic and Relevant; Time-bound and Trackable) goals, there's virtually no insight into what exactly people should be doing, and there's no way to determine whether the courses of action being taken are correct or need to be modified.

Contrary to what has all too often been published regarding the efforts required to produce these four cornerstones – values, vision, mission, and goals – the time expended pales in comparison to the time wasted when people aren't guided and supported by them.

> ☑ **Bring together the best people you can**
>
> ☑ **Solidify their collective identity**
>
> ☑ **Make sure they're able and willing to be a team**

Those who know do.

Those who know more do better.

Those who can best apply what they know excel.

What should I start doing, stop doing, do differently?

What effect(s) do I expect from these actions?

How will I know if the expected effect(s) occur?

BUILDING A SOLID TEAM

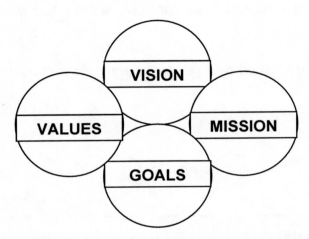

Once the foundation has been properly set, then team building can occur with the focus on developing necessary attributes.

Real teams understand that they're fundamentally different than a "collection of individuals" or a "group."

While a "collection of individuals" might all be wearing the same color tee shirts, and a "group" might have their group's name on their tee shirts, a "team" would likely have their collective identity as well as their individual identity on their tee shirts.

When I went to gym class (what I knew as phys ed), I went because I was scheduled to be with that particular "collection of individuals;" when I joined a running club it was to be associated with a "group," yet whenever I didn't appear, they could still go off for a great run; and when I was a starter on a basketball team, that "team" suffered when I was injured and could not participate.

To best test where your "collection," "group" or "team" might be on the continuum, ask yourself: "To what extent am I hearing the following being said?"

- We're all in this together, sharing information, accountability and consequences.
- We understand the whole process and everyone's role in it.
- We know everyone's strengths and weaknesses.
- We know how everyone likes to work best and support each other in developing new capabilities.
- We recognize that whoever is best qualified to be the "boss" at any point in time is the "boss."
- Our attitude is one of *want to* rather than *have to*, each of us providing time and energy, not just time, and being committed rather than compliant.
- We have a purpose that is consciously chosen by all, one that is clearly articulated, providing ongoing general direction and fulfillment, and one that is checked periodically to ensure relevance.
- We really communicate with each other, not judging or evaluating, and listen and respond to each other without prejudice or indifference.
- We live in the moment yet with an eye to the future, not getting stuck and always looking forward so that tactical initiatives become rolling strategic objectives.
- We avoid limited thinking, limited participation and "killer phrases" *("We tried that; it never works")* while always striving to get beyond perceived limitations.
- We're consensus driven – proposals are clear to everyone, concerns are resolved, questions are answered, and everyone agrees to support the decision reached.

- We recognize and accept what is our natural evolution:

FORMING: coming together

STORMING: the natural conflict associated with forming

NORMING: finding the pattern(s)/process(es)

PERFORMING: making the process(es) work

HIGH PERFORMING: perfecting the process(es)

TRANSFORMING: gaining/losing member(s)

REFORMING

We're adequately prepared for the inevitability of TRANSFORMING, and the subsequent need to REFORM, to prevent our team's regression.

When we meet, we are clear on our Goals *("Why are we meeting?")*, our Agenda *("What we'll be doing")* and the Benefits to be derived *("What's in it for me to attend/us to meet?")*.

In summary, real teams do not simply occur. They require the full abilities and willingness of every member to develop and sustain cohesiveness and interdependence, focused on a mutually agreed-upon set of goals and a never-ending commitment to collective results.

> ☑ *It's much more than wearing the same color tee shirts*
>
> ☑ *It's about always being prepared for transforming*
>
> ☑ *It's all about saying "we" even if you're alone*

Those who know do.

Those who know more do better.

Those who can best apply what they know excel.

What should I start doing, stop doing, do differently?

What effect(s) do I expect from these actions?

How will I know if the expected effect(s) occur?

PRESENTING TO A GROUP, TEAM OR OTHERS

According to the American Psychological Association, our greatest fear is speaking in public – *lalophobia* – yet, when we're "in-charge," we have little if any chance of avoiding the times we'll have to face it, and beat it.

Conquering the feelings of anxiety, inadequacy, stage fright and simple nervousness is relatively easy if you focus on your self-awareness and self-management.

I've coached literally hundreds of people who wanted to become better presenters, and in virtually every case, the improvements they realized were directly attributable to better managing their attitude and their self-talk.

Telling yourself PRIOR to presenting, "I am nervous, YET,

- I am intelligent
- I have a good vocabulary
- I am a caring person
- I am creative
- I am enthusiastic
- I know my material
- I have the ability to deliver a great talk…

and I am ready to begin now" is the best way to properly set the right mental tone for a great presentation.

Of course, to be a really great presenter, you must always be…

- **attention-getting** in your opening, because you've only got the first 60-120 seconds to grab hold of your audience

- giving your audience what they are there for: a **compelling reason to listen** to what you're about to say

- **meaningful** by providing the audience with more value than if they simply read your presentation

- **memorable** long after your delivery

- providing the **ways and means** for your audience to do what you want them to

- **grounded** in your content without using it to an excess

- **clear** in how you deliver the content

- **empathetic** and audience-centric, showing them you really care

- **open-minded** and **negotiable**, treating other points of view as though they are simply questions to be answered

- **responsive** to questions without forsaking your purpose

- **enthusiastic** and **engaging** through the vocal and visual elements of your presentation

- **as well prepared as possible**, and flexible and adaptable since "stuff happens."

Structurally, every great presentation is designed around the answers to 3 key questions:

1. "What do these people want/need to hear from me?"
   - facts and data and/or stories and opinions?
   - about the past, present and/or future?
   - how are they going to get there, and what's in it for them when they do?
2. "What connection do I have with these people?"
   - "have I walked in their shoes in some way at some time?"

- "are we in the same sandbox today?"
- "are they seeking my help, or am I here because I need/want their help?"

3. "What are the 3 key points I need/want to get across?"

- each connected to your opening, and each other
- with appropriate transitions ("bridges") between each
- each leading to your slam-bang conclusion

Of course, you do want to acknowledge that:

- 10% of every group doesn't want to be there (and it has nothing to do with you, so don't take it personally)
- 10% of every audience will likely think it has been a life-changing event if you do nothing but belch for an hour
- you really need to focus on the remaining 80%…get them going in the right direction and you're on your way.

Great presenters – people who can really deliver what an audience needs and wants to hear – are made, not born: Jack Welch and James Earl Jones, both of whom are controlled stutters, have captured the hearts and minds of many audiences during their storied careers.

Want to be great? Practice perfection!

☑ ***Tell people what it is that you're going to tell them***

☑ ***Then tell them***

☑ ***Then tell them what it was you told them***

Those who know do.

Those who know more do better.

Those who can best apply what they know excel.

What should I start doing, stop doing, do differently?

What effect(s) do I expect from these actions?

How will I know if the expected effect(s) occur?

MINIMIZING AND HANDLING CONFLICT

Conflict in every sandbox is inevitable!

According to the folks at The Leadership Development Institute at Eckerd College, the producers of the Conflict Dynamics Profile®, conflict is defined as "any situation in which people have incompatible goals, interests or feelings."

In further support of my inevitability claim, Charles Dana reported in "Conflict Resolution: Mediation Tools For Everyday Worklife" that "unmanaged employee conflict is responsible for 65% percent of work performance problems;" and Watson Hoffman reported in the Leadership Quarterly that "30-42% of a typical manager's time is spent dealing with conflict and its consequences."

Like I said, conflict is inevitable!

If you're directly involved in it:

- Be empathetic/sympathetic and try your best to understand the other person's point of view.
- Utilize the power of "the 8 magic words" imparted to me by Larry Wilson, author of <u>Changing The Game,</u> "I have a problem; I need your help," which amazingly seem to diffuse resistance when confronting someone.
- Brainstorm with the other person, ask questions, and try to create solutions to the problem.
- Talk honestly with the other person and express your thoughts and feelings.

- Reach out to the other person, make the first move, and try to make amends.
- Analyze the situation, weigh the pros and cons, and think about the best response.
- Wait things out, let matters settle down, or take a "time out" when emotions are running high.

If all your attempts fail, resign yourself to avoiding this person, or removing yourself from his/her presence and influence, checking to be certain that you'll be able to handle any collateral damage.

If you happen to be lucky enough to be one of those who is a "boss" of others in the sandbox, and are therefore spending upwards of "42% of your time dealing with conflict and its consequences," you have 3 ways to handle things, best done in a step-by-step fashion:

1.   Coach the parties so that they will be better able to resolve their own problem(s).

2.   Facilitate a meeting of the parties in which you ensure that the burden for the resolution remains in their hands.

3.   Resolve it for them, ensuring that the resolution you impose sticks.

To dramatically reduce the potential for conflict, use "positive confrontation" – the artful engagement with another party during which you are:

- hard on the problem, not the person(s)
- being "ask-assertive," questioning to determine what the underlying cause of this soon to be conflict-laden situation is
- and resolving it before it turns in that direction.

An even more proactive approach has you and others engaging in meaningful conversations where you candidly disclose your expectations of each other, down to the most minute details — *"I really prefer that you call me, not e-mail me, when discussing other people."* — which, when adhered to by the other party will likely remove the possibility of conflict ever occurring.

In summary, differences should not have to result in conflict. Developing relationships that are solidly based on mutual comfort, trust and respect should allow for "competitive dialogue" that airs views, issues and opportunities that would never injure any of the parties.

> ☑ **Positive confrontation minimizes conflict**
>
> ☑ **Be hard on problems, never on the person(s)**
>
> ☑ **Practice tolerance**

Those who know do.

Those who know more do better.

Those who can best apply what they know excel.

What should I start doing, stop doing, do differently?

What effect(s) do I expect from these actions?

How will I know if the expected effect(s) occur?

FACILITATING TRANSITION AND CHANGE

In the 16th century the great Florentine statesman Niccolo Machiavelli stated, "There is nothing more difficult to plan, more doubtful of success or more dangerous to manage than the introduction of a new order of things."

In the 19th century the great American poet, naturalist and essayist Henry David Thoreau said, "Things do not change; we change."

In the early 20th century, Prime Minister Winston Churchill said, "To improve is to change; to be perfect is to change often."

In the late 20th century, the noted writer and business consultant Tom Peters exclaimed, "Excellent firms don't believe in excellence – only in constant improvement and constant change."

All of these great thinkers and doers, through the ages, spoke of change in ways that make any of us stop for a moment and reflect on why and what it may be that makes "change" a topic that is constantly and continuously discussed.

For that you need travel back more than 2,200 years, to 252 B.C., to the time of Heraclitus, a Greek philosopher, for it is he who is credited with "Nothing endures but change," the first known articulation of the omnipresent modern-day mantra everyone recites: "The only thing that's constant in our lives is change!"

In my experience, most people use the word "change" synonymously with the word "transition," yet my work with individuals, groups and entire sandboxes has clarified an important distinction:

"change" is physical,

yet "transition" is psychological,

and transition can occur well before, and often lasts well after, the actual change takes place.

Stand around the water cooler after a hint of change is noticed and you'll find 80% of the people will have already begun to transition.

Whatever they may be anticipating, which is all too often more negative than positive, has set the wheels of acceptance, neutrality or resistance in motion well in advance of any of the actual effects of the impending change.

For change to succeed, the anticipated increase in performance with fulfillment (P+F) must be greater than the sum of the cost of maintaining the present state (TY) and creating the future state (TW), multiplied by the degree of acceptance (A) by those who have to implement the change. In formulaic terms:

$$\blacktriangle\uparrow(P+F) > C\ [(TY+TW)\ (A)]$$

To succeed – as a "boss," change agent, or follower – it is most important that:

- the proper attitude is created
- the proper behaviors be exhibited
- there's recognition that people can and will move through transition and the actual change at varying and perhaps different paces.

Think about thriving, not surviving, during times of change.

Focus on what's to be gained from the change, the compelling reason for the change and within the context of opportunity, seek out the benefits that can be realized.

Constantly move forward with flexibility and adaptability:

- proactively going into situations without preconceived notions

- reactively modifying your course of action, when necessary, without losing effectiveness.

See all that's changing for the opportunity it may provide.

Avoid focusing on what may be perceived losses resulting from the change; focus instead on what can be gained, and strive to make the most from every opportunity the change creates.

Empower everyone to be a positive agent for change, getting everyone to talk the talk and walk the walk.

If you happen to be involved in a change affecting others in your sandbox, find the early adopters and create an environment in which everyone is encouraged to be fully engaged and committed.

While changing, pick low-hanging fruit quickly, because success breeds success.

Look for small, easy wins that can be achieved quickly yet effectively, and take advantage of the opportunities to gain momentum as rapidly as possible.

Celebrate each and every success during times of change.

While it's easy to bemoan the constancy of change, it serves no useful purpose. Instead, take the time, with each move in a forward direction, to enjoy the achievement.

Get big steps from baby steps.

As is said in the ancient Indian proverb, "Never attempt to eat an entire elephant at one time." Change, even accelerated change, is best managed incrementally, in an evolutionary fashion, rather than in a revolutionary, cataclysmic fashion.

Minimize your time in between the old and the new – that period of time before or after you may have let go, yet you haven't moved on yet, so your feet are sort of planted firmly in midair – and do whatever you need do to move yourself forward, or even backward, as quickly as possible.

Tolerate discomfort, eliminate F•E•A•R.

Most people are naturally uneasy during times of change since they're moving out of their comfort zone.

Yet when people evidence F•E•A•R it is generally due to:

- avoidance (**For Ever Avoiding Reality**)
- insufficient info (**False Evidence Appearing Real**)
- true fright (**F___ Everything And Run**)

all of which are counter-productive.

Be patiently impatient, or impatiently patient, with yourself and with others, lest you move too quickly, or slowly.

Lastly, and in some ways most importantly, over-communicate, and when you do, be honest (truthful), candid (unconditional truth) and forthright (unqualified truth without being asked), because the failure to do so will fuel the rumor mill, and too often what people make up, whether they say it to themselves or others, is quite likely to be negative.

In summary, remember the immortal words spoken by Patrick Stewart in "The Winds of Change"..."Change can be a force to be feared, or an opportunity to be seized; the choice is in our hands."

☑ *Change = Different*

☑ *Nothing changes until something changes*

☑ *Change requires ability and willingness*

Those who know do.

Those who know more do better.

Those who can best apply what they know excel.

What should I start doing, stop doing, do differently?

```
┌─────────────────────────────────────────────────────┐
│                                                       │
│                                                       │
│                                                       │
│                                                       │
│                                                       │
│                                                       │
└─────────────────────────────────────────────────────┘
```

What effect(s) do I expect from these actions?

```
┌─────────────────────────────────────────────────────┐
│                                                       │
│                                                       │
│                                                       │
│                                                       │
│                                                       │
│                                                       │
└─────────────────────────────────────────────────────┘
```

How will I know if the expected effect(s) occur?

```
┌─────────────────────────────────────────────────────┐
│                                                       │
│                                                       │
│                                                       │
│                                                       │
│                                                       │
│                                                       │
└─────────────────────────────────────────────────────┘
```

FULFILLMENT SUSTAINS PERFORMANCE

From one of the most worthwhile texts ever written – <u>The Value Profit Chain</u> by James L. Heskett, W. Earl Sasser, Jr., and Leonard A. Schlesinger – I learned the true value of fulfillment: *"today's employee satisfaction, loyalty and commitment strongly influences tomorrow's customer satisfaction, loyalty and commitment and ultimately the organization's profit and growth."*

From this I concluded...

- It's always the people who come first.
- Happy people really are more productive.
- Commitment outperforms compliance every time.

Thanks to some incredibly valuable work done by the folks at the Gallup Organization, particularly Marcus Buckingham, and *Fast Company* magazine, I found a means for measuring people's fulfillment by allowing them to answer the following questions, in a brutally honest fashion, using a 1 (never) to 10 (always) scale:

1) To what extent do you know what is expected of you at work?

2) To what extent do you have the materials and equipment that you need in order to do your work properly?

3) To what extent do you have the opportunity to do what you do, to the best of your ability, every day at work?

4) To what extent have you received recognition or praise for your efforts or results in the last 30 days?

5) To what extent does your supervisor, or someone at work, seem to care about you as a person?

6) To what extent does someone at work actively encourage your development?

7) To what extent do your opinions seem to count at work?

8) To what extent does the mission or purpose of your company make you feel that your job is important?

9) To what extent are your coworkers committed to doing quality work?

10) To what extent are you comfortable with, and trusting and respectful of, the people with whom you work?

11) In the past month, how often has someone at work talked to you about your progress?

12) To what extent have you had opportunities to learn and grow at work in the last 6 months?

With a minimum score of 12, and a maximum of 120, it became easy to gauge individuals, teams and even entire sandboxes' fulfillment levels.

With that information in hand, I could ask people to also rate their own performance levels, or seek that data from others, ultimately to help determine what actions need to be taken to produce higher levels of commitment, efficiency and effectiveness.

Of course, once you've been able to raise levels of fulfillment, the work doesn't end, since sustaining them can certainly be just as challenging.

To that end, I'd recommend...

- Avoiding "Flavor of the Month Clubs" that seem to only produce very temporary up-ticks in fulfillment.
- Never accepting compliance (which can be acceptable at times) when commitment (the provision of both time AND energy, rather than just time) is possible.
- Recognizing the flip in the "psychological contract" that exists in the minds of sandboxers and employers: People no longer work for you, they work for themselves.
- That when you're thinking about initiating changes for the better, make certain that everyone in the sandbox knows why, what, how and when, because what people are most afraid of is that which they don't understand.

In summary, when people enjoy their endeavors – find satisfaction in the work they do, the people they're with and the environment in which they spend so much of their time – their willingness to be actively engaged no doubt increases and with it their performance.

> ☑ **The only way to measure fulfillment is to ask**
>
> ☑ **Higher fulfillment =**
> **Stronger commitment =**
> **Better performance =**
> **Ever-increasing results**

Those who know do.

Those who know more do better.

Those who can best apply what they know excel.

What should I start doing, stop doing, do differently?

What effect(s) do I expect from these actions?

How will I know if the expected effect(s) occur?

MOVING PEOPLE UP, OVER OR OUT

Moving people up or over generally requires two perspectives – short-term and longer-term – and two sets of needs – the individual who's moving and the sandbox's.

Regarding the perspectives, what with the rapidity that people move in today's sandboxes, consider the short-term as being defined in months (3-12), and longer-term any timeframe beyond that.

Regarding the individual's needs, make certain they're prepared to present them in a meaningful manner; that is, based on a brutally honest assessment of:

- What do I do best? *(my skills, abilities, strengths)*
- What do I like most? *(from what do I derive fulfillment?)*
- What's most important to me? *(things I value most).*

To the extent the opportunities in the sandbox can be aligned with the highest priority answers to all 3 questions, the greater the likelihood the person will not only want to stay, the more committed he/she will be.

Regarding the departure of people from the sandbox…

If they leave voluntarily, make certain to ask them two questions (in addition to whatever other exit interview questions you might ask):

1. What would have gotten you to stay?
2. Can we call you in 3 months to see how you're doing?

    (at which point you should ask them "Why did you actually leave?" and compare their answer(s) to what

you got in the exit interview: don't be surprised when you gain some invaluable information that may help curtail your future loss of people you would otherwise like to retain).

If you do actually need to jettison someone, ask yourself:

- Did I effectively communicate the job's task, goals and behavioral expectations?

- Did I give the sandboxer the benefit of deeply honest, fact-based feedback?

- Did I listen to learn and understand the sandboxer's problems?

- Did I supportively confront the sandboxer about the specific undesired behaviors?

- Did I precisely define what was not working?

- Did I provide appropriate forms of behavior modification to improve skill/increase willingness?

- Did I use appropriate methods of conflict resolution to address underlying issues?

Also consider:

- Is the rule or expectation this person violated clear and reasonable?

- Was the analysis of the facts fair and objective?

- Did the sandboxer know or should have known of the rule or expectation he/she violated?

- Is the evidence of noncompliance substantial?

- Has the rule or expectation been applied to all sandboxers equally, without discrimination?

- Was the sandboxer notified of the problem sufficiently?

- Did the sandboxer have a reasonable opportunity to correct the problem?

- Was the sandboxer properly supported in correcting the problem?

- Was the discipline progressive and incremental, moving from penalty to punishment, before termination?

- Did the discipline take into account the sandboxer's entire record?

- Was the discipline proportionate to the severity of the problem?

Once asked, and answered, then make certain to plan your next steps in conjunction with the sandbox's human resource professionals, people who are best qualified to ensure you do what you're entitled to do, properly.

> ☑ **People today are loyal to themselves**
>
> ☑ **Not everyone wants to be promoted**
>
> ☑ **Poor performers hurt everyone**

Those who know do.

Those who know more do better.

Those who can best apply what they know excel.

What should I start doing, stop doing, do differently?

What effect(s) do I expect from these actions?

How will I know if the expected effect(s) occur?

HELPING YOURSELF TO BETTER HELP OTHERS

A dear, dear friend, who was lost to me at much too early an age, would sit with me at times and remind us both that all too often "life sucks, and then you don't die."

People seem to always try so hard, often in vain, to get and keep all their lives – work, family, social, spiritual, communal – in balance, yet they generally end up not really enjoying any of them.

From my experience, personally and with others, there are three rules for dealing with this dilemma:

Rule #1:   Embrace the natural imbalance in life.

Really come to grips with whatever is your current reality … the sandbox you work in, and the world that you live in, such as it is, not the way you would like it to be.

Rule #2:   Always put your oxygen mask on first.

If you aren't at your best, at least 80% of the time, you're likely not going to get much enjoyment out of your life, and you're probably going to make everyone around you miserable as well.

Rule #3:   Enjoy what you do, and do what you enjoy.

Rather than struggling to incorporate and integrate everything, find those things that really do bring you, and the people you really care about, a greater sense of fulfillment, and make the most out of the time in your sandbox(es) to enjoy them.

Sit down one day, perhaps with a great single malt Scotch, or a Chateau Petrus, and answer the same questions you'd ask anyone you're helping with career/life decisions:

1.   What do you really do best?

2.   What do you really like most?

3.   What's really most important to you?

When you've exhausted all the answers to all 3, go back to each column and find the absolute top 3 choices; the next time you look at an opportunity, whether in your current sandbox or a new one, see how it matches up against your answers, rather than comparing it to what you're currently doing or otherwise contemplating.

On a somewhat more tactical level, always think about what you do at work with regard to value and priority.

- If something is high value and mission critical, then **do it**.

- If something is high value and there's time available, **delegate it.**

- If something is lesser value yet needed relatively soon, **delay it** with the understanding that there is a deadline looming.

- If something is of little value and there's no urgency whatsoever, **dump it**.

In summary, balancing your workload will not only help you to better deal with the natural imbalances of life, it will undoubtedly help you better engage and gain commitment from those whose efforts and results lend themselves to your fulfillment.

☑ *Be flexible and adaptable (see Chapter 2)*

☑ *Help yourself first (to best help others)*

☑ *Do what's important and jazzes you*

Those who know do.

Those who know more do better.

Those who can best apply what they know excel.

What should I start doing, stop doing, do differently?

What effect(s) do I expect from these actions?

How will I know if the expected effect(s) occur?

KNOWING THAT YOU'RE SUCCEEDING

- You're not focused on whether the glass is half-full or half-empty, but on how big the glass is, and what's in it.

- You're enjoying the achievement of the plans you've made.

- You're an active player in the game of life.

- You recognize the real value of active listening.

- You know it's true… "Oz never did give nothing to the Tin Man that he didn't already have." *(America, 1973)*

- You know where you're going and which road will get you there.

- You minimize errors by knowing what you need and minimize remorse by knowing what you want.

- You're "hard" on problems yet "soft" on people.

- You plan for the best, yet are prepared for the worst.

- You accept that being "in-charge" isn't being "in control."

- You know true joy having defined it for yourself.

- You're expending all your energy toward things that others will value and cherish when you're gone.

- You're doing all the right things right.

MOVING FROM KNOWING TO DOING

The previous 18 chapters hopefully have provided, enhanced, affirmed or reaffirmed the basics you need to succeed in your sandbox.

Yet like learning to play tennis or the piano, only perfect practice will develop your ability to apply what you know.

Of course, perfect practice will likely require the assistance of a skilled teacher/mentor to ensure that your knowledge is being properly applied.

To that end I invite you to contact me (michael@myriaddevelopment.net) or visit my website (www.myriaddevelopment.net) to discover the workshops, seminars and coaching services that are available to assist you in your continued growth and development.

ACKNOWLEDGEMENTS

Wherever possible I have tried to translate theory into application, based on what I have learned, observed, advocated and practiced. Additionally, whenever possible, I have brought forth concepts, notions, anecdotes and musings provided by the many who I have admired during my career, as well as from those who did the right things wrong, the wrong things right or the wrong things wrong.

I freely admit there are paraphrasings, interpretations and borrowings from numerous sources, not all of which have been properly attributed, and to you I offer my most profound apologies. I ask that when you see/hear your words, you'll take pride in knowing they are being used in search of the greater good by all who read them.

To the many teachers, mentors, clients and colleagues who shaped my thinking, I offer my appreciation.

To the many friends who encouraged me to write, I offer my sincere gratitude.

To my wonderful family – wife Janet and daughters Jennifer and Alaina – I offer my heartfelt thanks for your never-ending support.

ABOUT THE AUTHOR

Michael Crystal has been employed and engaged by more than 50 of the FORTUNE 500, as well as a multitude of not-for-profit and public sector leader/managers and organizations, spending more than 30 years helping them perform better.

In addition to his extensive practical experience, he holds degrees in psychology, industrial management and organizational behavior, and has pursued the advanced study of individual and organizational development at Stanford, Harvard and Columbia universities, the Cape Cod Institute and the Gestalt International Study Center.

A member of Who's Who in Finance and Industry and Who's Who Amongst Human Services Professionals, he is also an affiliate member of the APA's Society of Consulting Psychology. Additionally, he is a professor at Manhattanville College's Graduate School for Professional Studies, has been a keynote speaker at numerous industry and company-sponsored events, and a guest lecturer at the University of Michigan Graduate School of Business Executive Education Program.

An "Expressive Baby-Boomer," he resides and practices in Wilton, CT.